CaN wE TaLk, LoRD?

prayers from a teenager's heart

DaVID GaTwaRD

Kevin
Mayhew

First published in 1998 by
KEVIN MAYHEW LTD
Rattlesden
Bury St Edmunds
Suffolk IP30 0SZ

0 1 2 3 4 5 6 7 8 9

ISBN 0 86209 223 X
Catalogue No 1440302

Cover design by Jaquetta Sergeant
Edited by David Gatward
Typesetting by Louise Selfe
Printed and bound in Great Britain

Contents

Acknowledgements

The Big 'G': Thanks, God, for absolutely everything!

Dad: For all the encouragement . . . and the occasional kick.

Mum: See? Your number 1 son isn't doing too bad!

John and James: Not just brothers, but my best mates. Cheers.

Stage II: Keep in touch, eh?

My Church (too many people to mention): for your love and support over the years.

Shaz: For being there from the beginning.

Ray and Chris: For the encouragement, friendship and wine!

Grant: Thought it was about time I mentioned you!

*To Mum and Dad
and my two brothers,
John and James.
This book is for you.*

Foreword

I remember being eleven and saying to Mum that I wanted to be a writer when I grew up. She patted me on the head, smiled, said, 'That's nice dear!' and that was that. I suppose it was a bit like having me say, 'I want to be a pop star!' Not exactly the kind of safe career you want your children to pursue! yet, here I am, a fair number of books behind me and perhaps some more in front, too. Amazing!

I wrote all these prayers between the ages of sixteen and eighteen, so they were basically about what I was going through at the time – being a teenager, not wanting to go to college, having spots, failing exams, girlfriend problems, etc, etc! I look back at them now and it's a bit like looking at an old diary. I sometimes find it hard to believe that the thoughts were even mine! But the reason I wrote them was simple; it was me and God talking about life and stuff and stuff and life.

The prayers were never written to be published, it just happened that way, which is perhaps why they have been so well received. They aren't perfect, they aren't great literature, but they are real.

Now, a few years on, I've added a little bit extra by way of a small introduction to each prayer. Hopefully they'll make you think a bit, laugh a bit and perhaps even pray a bit! Hope you like them.

DAVE

My family

Intro bit . . .

The 'family' isn't such a straight cut idea any more, is it? To be honest, I don't think it ever was. Take one look at black and white photographs of stuffy Victorians and I think you'll see what I mean; all this 'children shall be seen and not heard'! What a load of rubbish!

But 'God's Family' is different. It's about everyone, regardless of status. And that's what I like about God. We're all part of his family and he accepts us as we are. Shouldn't we, therefore, follow his example with each other, even if perhaps, we've never even met?

Praying bit . . .

Lord, you there?
It's about my family.
I've been thinking about them
    for a while now.

What is it?
Why is it?
Who is it?

First, there's my 'real' family.
Mum,
    Dad,
      two brothers,
        and a mixed bag of relatives!
Lord, I love them all!
Thanks for my family;

they're the best,
they've helped me so much.

We've had our problems,
our arguments.
But the tears
always gave way to smiles,
and laughter,
and happiness.
Thanks, Lord!

And then,
there's my wider family;
those 'out there'.
Not just the Church, Lord,
though I am grateful for it,
for the Christian family,
my friends back at church,
and in the youth group.

But it's the wider family
that's on my mind,
the ones really 'out there'.
For they too are my brothers, and sisters,
and your children.

The homeless,
the hungry,
the poverty stricken,
and the terminally ill.
The Aids sufferers,
the disadvantaged,
the junkies,
and those who, for whatever reason,
are locked away.

The list is endless, Lord.
So many unhappy people,
    and so many of them
    who don't know you.

And all of them
    are my brothers,
    my sisters,
    your children.

It hurts, Lord.
It hurts to see my family in such a mess,
    to see it spoiled,
    so torn apart by hate,
    misunderstanding,
    a lack of trust,
    a famine of love.

Lord,
    Father,
    I thank you for what I have.
Please forgive me
    for so often forgetting
    how fortunate I am,
    and for ignoring those
    who do not have
    what I have.
Those with no family,
    no friends,
    no love,
    no you!

Help my brothers and sisters, Lord,
    your children.

Amen.

Lord, can we talk?

I wrote most of these prayers aged sixteen to eighteen, and, though that's not that long ago, some really make me cringe! This is one of them! Let me introduce myself . . . I'm Mr Romantic Disaster!

The whole boyfriend/girlfriend thing is such a major part of teenage life (and the rest of it!) I wonder sometimes why people aren't a little bit more understanding. From romantic bliss to break-up hell, it isn't exactly easy.

But the Bible says God understands, and I think he does. Why? Well, Jesus was young once too . . .

Praying bit . . .

Lord, can we talk?
I feel daft praying about this again
    but I feel I've got no one else to talk to –
    just you.

It's girls again!
That time-old problem.
What am I going to do, Lord?
I'm so confused.
It's so painful knowing what I could do
    if I were home.

But I'm not!
I'm here,
    a hundred miles away
    from a very special person.
It's not fair, God!

Remember her letter?
And how about when we said
    'goodbye'?
'Go and find someone good enough
    for you', she said.
For goodness sake!
I was saying goodbye to her!
The person good enough for me;
    now gone!

She hasn't even written.
Can't blame her really.
After my last letter,
    and knowing now how I feel.

God, why?

Come on, Lord,
    would you write?
I gave her no choice I guess.
Went out on my own
    before consulting you.

But I love her!
(At least I think I do!)
What I'd do given half the chance.
If only I knew how to make her love me!
But I don't.
And even if I did, no use it'd be,
    being here.

I'm a victim of geography.
I've lost again, God,
    I've lost again!
And I don't know what to do;
    I daren't write,

13

I daren't 'phone.
I'm so screwed up.
What chance is there for anything
    with a hundred mile gap?

All through the others
    I knew deep down how I really felt,
    yet I had to spend two years,
    helping her through!
Holding myself back from reaching out.

Lord, you know how I really fell for her.
Good grief, even Mum and Dad could tell!
'Hang in there', I get told.
'It depends how much you want her.'
But, Lord, all I can do is sit and cry!
Cry about a friendship.
One that became
    the centre of my life,
    one I so wanted to develop
    into something more.
It was never given a chance.

But even though I 'may' have lost a girlfriend
    (and the 'may' is in your hands, Lord!),
I gained the greatest,
    most caring,
    understanding,
    and lovely person
    as a friend.

Thank you, Lord.

Amen.

Lord, I've a few questions

Intro bit . . .

I haven't changed that much since writing these prayers. I'm a bit older, a bit more stupid, sorry, *wise*, and still full of questions. I'm an ordinary bloke trying to make sense of life and not getting it right all that often. But then God loves me the way I am! He loves ordinary people! He isn't amazed by the impressive qualities we look for in others, he's impressed by the amazing qualities he's found in us! Fantastic!

Praying bit . . .

> Lord, you got a minute?
> It's just that I've a few questions – again!
> This week's been quite good, Lord, really.
> (Not 'boring' as I'd expected!)
> Making friends, learning, talking.
> Great stuff.
> But there's this problem.
>
> I may be paranoid,
>   but it seems to me
>   that everyone else
>   has more to offer
>   than I do!
>
> Those with the 'rock-solid' faith.
> The ones who know the Bible
>   from cover to cover.
> Those who don't mind saying
>   what they think.

And me?
Well exactly . . . me?!
Come on, Lord, are you crazy?
I'm a clown, a long-haired idiot!
My faith has so many holes in it
    you could use it as a sieve!
I lose my temper,
    get angry if someone disagrees with me.
And to be honest, Lord,
    I find the Bible quite boring.
So what on earth *can* I offer?

Maybe I'm not the only one
    who feels like the worst Christian
    in the world.

Look at Peter.
He was a hot-headed fisherman
    with a tendency to speak first,
    and think later.
He even denied you three times.
Yet look what you did with him!

But that's you isn't it, Lord?
You like ordinary people.
You were a carpenter,
    your disciples,
    fishermen, tax collectors,
    and now me!

And for that, Lord, I thank you.
Thank you for choosing me,
    and for accepting me
    as I am.

Amen.

Lord, are you there?

If I had a penny for every time I've said, 'Lord, are you there?' I'd have oooh, rather a lot of pennies! It's one of my most common sentences. No matter what's going on or how good life may be, I still doubt. Daft? Well, not really. Human? Yes, very. I am human, I have flaws, but I have God as well. At times it seems that he's so very, very far away but then at times I guess God feels the same way about me.

Praying bit . . .

> Lord, are you there?
> It's just that I'm on my own
> > and I need someone
> > to talk to.
>
> (You don't mind if we have a chat,
> > do you, Lord?)
>
> I've just moved out, left home.
> It's kind of strange really.
> You can't go downstairs
> > and expect someone to be there,
> > watching TV
> > and ready for a chat.
>
> There's no vast pool of friends
> > to call on,
> > the church is strange,
> > people are strange,

you're suddenly on your own.
You say to yourself, 'It'll be fine'.
Convince yourself nothing can shake you.
Tell your family,
'Don't worry, I'll be OK.'

I'm not saying I'm depressed, Lord,
    or totally friendless or lonely.
It's just that it's a bit of a shock
    to the system.

It's so weird
    being away from home.
I keep running the fact I've left home
    over and over
    in my mind.

How did you feel
    when you left home, Lord?
Did you feel lonely?

Lord, this brings up the thought
    of your call to us.
You said we have to leave our families,
    take up our cross
    and follow you.

Do you know how hard that is, Lord?
My family mean so much to me.
They've helped me so much.
And my friends have, too.
Some of them are so very special.
I can't cope if I lose touch with them.

My social life,
    my hobbies,
    my life.

Lord, don't you think
   it's too much
   to ask?
To give up everything for you?
How can I, Lord?
How?

David, listen to me!
I gave up everything.
I was rejected in my home town.
I was betrayed
   by one of my closest friends.
I was denied three times.
They couldn't even stay awake for me.
And then I died, David.
I died for you!
I died so that you could know me.
I will never leave you, David.
I will always be by your side,
   because I love you.
So I ask you to follow me.

Amen.

Dreams

Intro bit . . .

This was an attempt at poetry and I still quite like it! A bit pretentious perhaps (moi?), but there's a lot of truth in it, I think. You see, I've always been a dreamer. I've never been content with the ordinary or the mundane or the expected. I can't help it and I'm proud of that! You see, dreams don't necessarily come from us, but from God. Perhaps he places these things in our minds so that we will always strive for something more, always push ourselves to be better than we already are. That's what dreaming and having dreams is all about! And the best thing about dreams? Some of them come true . . .

Praying bit . . .

> Life depends on dreams;
>> the ambitions of the heart,
>> that private yearning for something special.
>
> Yet once caught
>> they are like china in your hand,
>> beautiful but fragile, and easily broken.
>
> But if we shy away from our dreams,
>> afraid of losing something we so cherished,
>> we will never realise the beauty
>> of something that was truly and uniquely ours,
>> no matter how short lived.
>
> A life of dreams is better than a life of regrets.
> Grasp them while you can and hold them tight,
>> for tomorrow they may be gone.
>
> Amen.

Confused

Intro bit . . .

I still am and I'm sure I always will be! It's a natural trait of mine. You give me something to think about and I guarantee that within minutes I'll be confused.

You're probably the same. After all, life is hardly easy. But then I don't think it was meant to be. Too much of 'easy' and we get bored very quickly and that's not good. Perhaps confusion is healthy! Now there's a thought – it gets you thinking about things, makes you work them out, makes you keep striving for something. Excellent! I'm confused and it's not a bad thing! Thanks, God!

Praying bit . . .

> You got a minute, Lord?
> It's about being, well, er,
>   kind of,
>   confused.
>
> Everything and nothing
>   is happening at the same time!
> Decisions to be made,
>   work to be done,
>   problems to be solved.
>
> Do you understand, Lord?
> You see, it's not so much a case of being lost,
>   more of a 'spaghetti junction' in life.
> Where do I go, Lord?
> Where are the signposts?
> Which road do I follow?
> I've so much I want to do, yet so little I can.

Are my thoughts clouded, Lord?
Sometimes I despair.
It just doesn't seem worth it.
I want to run, Lord, get away.
From you, friends, work, life.
Everything.
Is it worth carrying on, Lord?
I see no light at the end of the tunnel.
Where are you in this swirling darkness?
Are you testing me, Lord?

It's at times like these
   that I need you most,
Yet . . . I get no answer.

I don't want to be rude, Lord, but . . .
   do you really exist?
It seems that logically you don't exist,
   yet at the same time you do!
You know what I mean, Lord?
Do you really understand?
Are you confused?
I really wonder sometimes, Lord,
   whether,
    well you know, what if?
Perhaps . . .
Why?
If only!!
CONFUSED!!

Oh, Lord, help me to untangle
the lines of my thoughts,
to see your purpose for me ahead.
I don't want to be confused any more, Lord.
It's confusing!!

Amen.

Alone

Intro bit . . .

No matter how old or young you are, feeling alone is probably one of the most heartbreaking situations to be in, and being a Christian doesn't necessarily make it any easier, no matter what some people say.

I'm not going to give you any wishy-washy advice like, 'Even Jesus felt alone' since, when you feel alone, you don't really care! I know I didn't. I just kept going, refusing to give in! Because of that, maybe I'm a little bit stronger than I used to be. Perhaps through the pain we grow, learning more than we realise about God and ourselves.

Praying bit . . .

> Lord, can't you hear me?
> Don't you hear my cry of pain?
> Are you there, in the darkness?
> Don't you know the way I feel?
>
> *David, I am here!*
>
> Lord, I am lost, can't you find me?
> I'm knocking, Lord,
>   why won't you answer?
> I'm alone, Lord,
>   why won't you comfort me?
> I'm hurt, why won't you heal?
>
> *David, I am here!*

Lord, I don't know which way to turn.
I'm alone, lost, and confused.
The love I seek is gone.
Where are you, Lord?

David, I am here!

Help me, Lord!
The darkness, it surrounds me!
I scrabble in the dust, alone on my knees.
My heart has been pierced,
    and my love rejected.
My life seems in ruins.
Won't you help me?

David, I am here!
My hand is outstretched for you!
I love you and will never leave you!
Why won't you listen?
Why won't you trust?
How weak your faith is!

I am HERE!

Lord?
Is that you?

Amen.

Prayer

Intro bit . . .

I've got seven prayer books to my name now and I still don't find prayer any easier! Why? Oh, the usual; too much to say, don't know how to say it, not enough time, and so on.

The only really important thing about prayer is that you have some. It may not be much or it may be hours long, but whatever it is, God wants to hear it. After all, if God doesn't get to hear you in this life, how's he going to recognise you in the next?

Praying bit . . .

> Lord, it's about prayer.
> Well, it's just I don't know how to . . .
>   well, you know,
>   pray.
>
> What is it, Lord?
> How do you start?
> What do you pray about?
> Who do you pray to?
> God?
> Jesus?
> Father?
> Mother?
> Lord?
> Dad?!!
>
> It's not easy, you know.
> There's never been any real guide
>   to follow.

'101 Ways to Pray!!'
Not a bad idea really is it?

It's all very well
   this Christian stuff,
    but how do you go about it?
Can't you give us
   even a tiny hint?

You say we should listen,
   but how can we do that
    when our minds are so full up
   we just forget to pray,
    never mind listen!

How do we know if you've heard us?
How do we know
   if we've been answered?
Do you understand, Lord?

It isn't just me, is it?
I often wonder
   if I'm the only Christian
    doing everything the wrong way!
But is there a wrong way, Lord?
Is there any way?

Bear with me, Lord.
It's tough
   but please keep helping me.
Even though I find it all so hard,
   I know I'd be lost without you.

You know what I really mean,
   even if my prayers don't say it.
You know what I need,
   not what I think I need.

Help me to trust your decision, Lord,
   even though it might hurt.
Pick me up
   when I fall down.
Heal my broken faith
   when I begin to doubt.
Teach me to pray, Lord.
Please!

Amen.

Parents

Intro bit . . .

Well, what are they? I mean, where do they come from? And where on earth do they buy their clothes?! I remember when I left home thinking that I'd be free at last and be able to do what I wanted. I don't think I've ever been so wrong! They always seemed to know more about what I was doing than I did!

And do you know what? That's actually quite a nice feeling . . .

Praying bit . . .

Hi, Lord!
Got a minute?

Well,
    it's about parents.
What *are* they, Lord?
One minute you hate 'em,
    next you love 'em!

'I've been there too,' they say.
Have they?
Are you sure they're not made
    in a 'parent factory'?
A huge production line,
    each given the necessary items
    for parenthood.
Yet, if that's so,
    why do they seem so incompetent
    when it comes to us,
    the 'adolescents'?

Are we that hard to understand, Lord?
Surely parents are there to help.
Then why do they always seem
    to hinder,
    never understand,
    jump to conclusions,
    and treat you like a child?
I thought they'd 'been there'!

Do you know what I mean, Lord?
They shout and scream at you, saying:
'I wonder if it's worth it', or,
    'I wouldn't have got away with that
    when I was your age!'

Teach them to listen, Lord.
To understand.
We know we're not perfect,
    but a little love
    and encouragement
    go a long way.

We know they love us, Lord,
    we really do.
Without them we'd never pull through.
    just let them know, Lord,
    how we feel.
And that although we find life difficult,
    we still love them,
    and always will.

Amen.

Growing up

Intro bit . . .

I've tried to do this, I really have, but I just can't get the hang of it! No matter what I do, 'growing up' is always an unattractive option.

One of the best things Jesus ever said (and he said quite a few) was that unless we became like children we would never enter the gates of heaven. Now I know there are lots of very deep meanings behind this but at the same time I think Jesus was making another more obvious point. As we grow up, we tend to forget what it was like to be a child. We forget all the craziness and the daft things we did. We forget that sense of discovery and wonder that we had about absolutely everything. We seem happier mowing lawns than getting down on our hands and knees to look past the grass and into the eyes of creepy crawlies.

We are God's children, so let's start acting a little bit more that way!

Praying bit . . .

> Lord, I'm alone,
>   alone in my room.
> Shut off from the turmoil
>   of the outside world.
> The only sound the soft,
>   calculated ticking
>   of my clock.
>
> It gives me time, Lord,
>   to gather my thoughts;
> The problems of teenage life . . .
>   adolescence.

It's strange, Lord, being seventeen.
Not an adult
    and not a child,
    yet expected to be one or the other
    several times a day.

Have adults forgotten
    that they were teenagers once?
Surely they should be filled with advice
    and help?
Yet all they do
    is shout
    and tell you to 'grow up'.

What is 'growing up', Lord?
If it means becoming like them,
    I don't want to.
They've stopped growing, Lord.
They think they've arrived,
    with no more to learn.
I don't want to be like that, Lord.

I want to be 'growing up'
    not a 'grown up'.
I never want to stop learning.
I want to remember what it's like
    being a teenager,
    and be able to understand
    how they feel.
I don't want to forget,
    like so many of the grown-ups today.

Why don't they understand, Lord?
Do we frighten them?
Are they scared of us?
We only want to be heard, Lord,

understood . . .
loved . . .

Don't they realise that, Lord?
Are they blind?

I don't think it's us
    that need help, Lord –
    it's them.

Amen.

I want

Intro bit . . .

We all say this, don't we? I know I do about pretty much everything.
I want to do well, I want to be liked, I want to be fit and healthy,
I want to be famous . . . The list is endless and probably rather
dull. God must get rather sick of my 'I want' prayers. After all, I don't
talk to my other friends and say, 'I want you to help me. I want
you to give me a sign that proves you're my friend!' and so on.

But 'I want' isn't necessarily a selfish statement. It doesn't
have to have anything to do with things for me. It can, though,
have a lot to do with things for you, and you, and you . . .

Praying bit . . .

Lord, I just want to apologise.
I'm sorry for wanting.
Every time I pray, it's all 'I want'.
And the things I want
    are usually so trivial,
    unimportant,
    unnecessary.

This time I want –
    to stop wanting!
I want to stop asking.

Prayer's supposed to be more
    than a list of requests
    that leave me angry
    when I don't get
    what I ask for.

What am I doing, Lord?
For not only am I upset
    when I don't get what I want,
    but then I forget to say
    'thanks', when I do!

Why do you bother?
You must get sick
    of being unappreciated.
I'm sorry.

Lord,
    help me to stop asking,
    to stop wanting,
    to just trust.
If I 'need' something,
    as long as you think I do
    then I know I'll get it.
And, Lord, if I don't,
    help me to understand why;
    why you said, 'No'.

And finally, Lord,
    help me to be
    what you want me to be.
And not what I want to be.

Amen.

Christmas!

Intro bit . . .

Well, I really was trying to be clever here, wasn't I? But that's what happens to us writers . . .

The sentiments are for real, though. Christmas; a time for giving and sharing and celebrating the birth of Jesus is now so commercialised that it wouldn't be difficult to believe that everyone was having a couple of days off simply to celebrate the existence of a certain soft drink!

It's no wonder that cynicism exists when, amongst all the glitter, we see people sleeping rough on our streets, living in dire poverty, going hungry, living outside of love. But it's into that world, that street, that alleyway, that Jesus went and calls us to follow . . . and even more so at Christmas.

Praying bit . . .

> On the first day of Christmas
>   my true love sent to me . . .
>   four bars of chocolate,
>   a large turkey,
>   three Christmas puddings,
>   and a huge iced Christmas cake!
>
> On the second day of Christmas
>   I saw a picture from Ethiopia
>   of a family starving in the hot desert.
> Their tired legs worn out
>   after many miles of walking
>   in search of food.
> Yet still their bowls are empty.

On the third day of Christmas
    my true love sent to me . . .
a new television
and a CD player.

On the fourth day of Christmas
    I turned on my television
    and saw a picture of a polluted river,
    its swirling mass carrying before it
    the decaying matter from everything
    it had touched.
The fish, birds, and plants
    that were once so attractive,
    now gone forever.

On the fifth day of Christmas
    my true love sent to me . . .
a chain made of gold,
and a ring of silver.

On the sixth day of Christmas
    I walked past a queue
    outside the Job Centre.
So many people wanting to work,
    to earn some money,
    when no jobs are available.

On the seventh day of Christmas
    my true love sent to me . . .
a card wishing 'good health,
and cheer for the New Year'.

On the eighth day of Christmas
    I walked past a young girl on the streets
    wrapped in a sleeping bag
    and huddled inside a brown
    cardboard box.

On the ninth day of Christmas
my true love sent to me . . .
a song she had written,
expressing her love for me.

On the tenth day of Christmas
two young children walked by
me in the street;
no shoes on their feet,
their clothes tattered and torn.
Who was giving them the love
they needed this Christmas?

On the eleventh day of Christmas
my true love sent to me . . .
a picture of the baby Jesus
in the stable, with Mary and Joseph
looking adoringly at him.

On the twelfth day of Christmas
I sat down and cried.
I cried for all who went without
this year.
No love,
no warmth,
no home,
no family,
no food.

Why *am* I celebrating Christmas?

And then I remembered . . .
a cross,
and an empty tomb.
I remembered a baby
coming as Light

into a world of cold, uncaring darkness.
A child of hope and peace,
   a child of salvation.
The Son of God,
   born for me,
   born for all!
A child to become the man
   who could change all things
   and all people!

Amen.

Memories

I love memories! Looking through old photos and laughing at the things we've done. Great stuff!

One thing I find is that when I look back on my (as yet) short life, I know that there have been bad times, but they pale into insignificance when compared to the good! Some memories still make me laugh out loud! Like the time my brother substituted mashed potato and gravy for the streamers in a party popper! I don't think I've ever laughed so much in my life! (Although my other brother wasn't too impressed with the spray of food that shot across the table and on to his shirt after grace!)

It's this thought, that I know there are good times to come, that often keeps me going through bad times. As one poet said (can't remember who!), 'I lost everything I ever loved, but still I was alive!' Now that's great, isn't it? To have life, to still have that opportunity to make something of yourself! Fantastic!

Praying bit . . .

> Lord, can you remember
>   my first attempt
>   at riding a bike?
> Yes, I know!
> I rode into a wall!
>
> A long time ago that, Lord,
>   a long time ago.
> Memories . . . what strange things.
> Happy times,
>   sad times,
>   some almost forgotten.

39

It's strange looking back.
I can sit for hours just remembering,
    looking through old photos,
    newspaper cuttings.
The occasional tear
    trickling down my cheek.

Looking back, Lord,
    my life has been pretty great so far.
I've done so much already.
There are periods I can remember
    which were tough;
    sitting there
    wondering why everything
    was going wrong.
Yet those times, Lord,
    I now realise
    were necessary,
    each one allowing me to develop
    in a different way.
To grow up a little,
    and learn a bit more.

Then there are the happy times!
Lord, I can never thank you enough
    for the happiness
    that has filled my life.
Just thinking about it
    makes me smile,
    and even laugh
    at some of the things I did!

You know, Lord,
    I think I can almost see
    a faint smile appear on your face, too!
A warm, happy,
    reminiscing smile.

You can remember too,
    can't you, Lord?
Do you remember those days in Galilee?
Sunny days, down by the lake?
Childhood days in Nazareth?
I'd give anything
    to know about that part
    of your life.

Did you get into trouble?
Did you get told off?
And, if you don't mind me asking, Lord,
    did you have girl trouble?

Yes, Lord, I knew I could see a smile.
You can remember!
Happy times and sad times.
That life so long ago.

Did you ever think
    you'd have such an effect?
Can you still remember
    your death, Lord?
When the nails
    tore through your wrists?
    when they hung you up,
    and you looked down
    on your mother,
    knowing you were going to die?
Do you remember it, Lord?
Do you?

Yes, David, I remember.
I remember the pain,
    the crown of thorns,
    the thought of dying.
I even remember the feeling

of the burning sun upon my back,
and the look on my mother's face
as I hung there.

Yes, David, I remember it.
I can remember every bead of sweat,
    every ounce of pain,
    every drop of blood,
    from that terrible day.
My hands still clench
    as I remember the nails.

But, David,
    I also remember why I died,
    why I suffered.
I died for you, David.
Remember?

Amen.

Boy meets girl

Intro bit . . .

Falling in love, going out, holding hands, snogging . . . the words
'run away!' can often enter the mind at this point! I'm an expert
at messing things up in this area. Don't ask me why, it's just a gift
I guess. Yet it is something that features so much in all our lives,
whether at school, college or work. There is a pressure on us all
to be with someone, find someone, get married, blah, blah, blah.
But it's not that easy; love never is. Risking love and acceptance
and happiness is risking rejection and hurt and pain, but that's
part of the deal. It's also part of the deal God took with us in giving
us free will. We have the freedom to do what we want, to choose
between right and wrong. Imagine how hurt God must feel when
we choose wrong. But then again, imagine how happy he must
be when he hears from you, finding his love returned!

Praying bit . . .

> Lord, are you there?
> Have you got time for a chat?
> Well, I just need to talk;
>   talk about a problem.
> It's not just mine though.
> I guess all teenagers (and adults!)
>   find it hard;
>   the dreaded first date,
>   the first kiss . . .
>
> Lord, why is it so hard?
> And not just the first time,
>   but *every* time?

How do you approach someone
    of the opposite sex?
How do you let them know
    you're interested
    without coming on too strong?
How do you know
    if they're interested in you?
And why does it seem easier
    for everyone other than me?!

Good grief, Lord,
    take it from me,
    this boy/girl stuff is agony!
One minute you're in love,
    next minute you hate each other!
Then, you just about get it together,
    and suddenly you've left home,
    and there's no chance!

Isn't it strange
    how this person
    seems to be the one for you,
    without whom you'd die
    of a broken heart,
    unable to go on!

Couldn't you make it easier, Lord?
You know, actually *tell* us
    if it is the right one,
    or if we actually stand a chance?
It's all so hit and miss.
(I'm not the only one
    who feels like this,
    am I, Lord?)

I know I'm asking a bit too much,
    and I'm sorry.

If I'm honest,
    I have to admit
    that even though a lot of pain
    and heartache is involved,
    it's still exciting!
In fact, a lot of it is good fun!
When it does work out,
    even for a short time,
    it's fantastic!

Lord, thank you for giving me
    the ability to survive
    the turmoils of teenage love.
Give me the courage and strength
    to keep going.
Help me to get better
    at this 'game of love'.

Finally, Lord,
    I pray that when I do find 'the one',
    you will be there
    to keep us together,
    and to help it last.

Amen.

Where am I?

Intro bit . . .

You know what? I still don't know; I haven't got a clue! I thought that by the time I hit twenty five I'd at least have some idea, but not so. Mind you, I can look back and see where I've been and that really is amazing! Which makes me question why I always want to know where I am, because God knows and, if I trust in him, surely that is all that matters.

Praying bit . . .

> Lord, remember when I was five?
> When I got lost in the supermarket?
> I wanted Mum and Dad,
>   wanted to go home.
>
> Like now.
> I'm not in a supermarket though,
>   I'm just lost.
>
> Where am I?
> Where do I go?
> What do I do?
> Why is life so confusing?
> Why do I keep getting lost?
>
> Are you there, Lord?
> Sometimes I even lose you,
>   or that's the way it seems.
> I wander off on my own.
> I 'know the way',

or that's what I imagine,
and I forget to ask you,
'Where do I go?
Which way do I take?'

Lord, help me to stop getting lost,
and help me to find my way home,
to you.

Amen.

Honesty

Intro bit . . .

Being honest with yourself is hard, not least because you can hurt yourself, and even hurt others too. If I'm honest, I don't like the kind of Christian I am. I'm a hypocrite, a scum bag, a liar, a cheat, a scaredy cat, a fake . . . but I still hold on. I can't do anything else. In being honest with myself about what I am and what I'm not, I find that I need that hand of God no matter what I've done or who I am. That is honesty – to be at the very, very bottom but still know in your heart of hearts that you need God, that you love him and that he will always, *always* love you.

Praying bit . . .

> Lord, it's about being honest . . .
>> and, to be honest,
>> I don't know where to start.
> Honesty can be good, and bad.
> It can get you into trouble,
>> lose you friends,
>> leave you standing on your own.
> For example, Lord,
>> say I didn't like someone . . .
>> does that mean I tell them?
> That's being honest isn't it?
> What if I see a tramp steal a hamburger
>> because he'd had nothing to eat
>> for a couple of days . . .
>> do I turn him over?
>
> You know, Lord,
>> I think a few guidelines on this
>> would have been useful.

When to be honest.
How to be honest.
Being honest to yourself.
The pros and cons of honesty.
Ever considered it?

Do I sound a bit confused, Lord?

I'm not really . . . well, not much.
I think my real problem
    is about being honest
    with myself.
I'm not the wonderful guy
    I like to think I am.
I'm not full of confidence,
    and I'm definitely not
    happy all the time.
In fact, Lord,
    I don't even consider myself
    to be a good example
    of Christianity.
I look at myself
    and often don't like what I see.
I'm not good enough
    to be associated with you, Lord.
To be honest, I find it hard to
    understand why you love me.

But, Lord,
    that's why I keep coming back.
Being honest with myself
    is admitting I can't survive without you.
I need you every hour of every day.
Please stay with me, Lord.
I need you, I honestly do!

Amen.

Saying sorry

Intro bit . . .

Not easy, is it, saying sorry? Especially when you know that it's not you who should be saying sorry. But so what? Sorry isn't about whose fault it is, it's about admitting that you're not perfect but that you still care. That's what 'saying sorry' is truly about.

Praying bit . . .

> Lord, you there?
> I need a bit of help.
> It's about saying sorry.
> In the words of Elton John:
> 'Sorry seems to be the hardest word'.
>
> Why is it, Lord?
> It's easy enough to pronounce,
>   easy to spell,
>   takes very little energy to say.
> So, where's the problem?
>
> It's not saying it
>   that's the problem, though,
>   is it, Lord?
> It's the reason for saying it.
> The accepting that you're wrong,
>   the fact that you have to admit to someone
>   that you have to say sorry to them.
>
> It hits home, Lord,
>   damages your self-image,

your pride, your confidence,
your credibility.

And therein lies the problem – PRIDE.
Too proud to say 'sorry'.
I wonder how many friendships
    have been spoilt
    because someone was too proud
    to say, 'I'm sorry'.
Just how many marriages
    would still be going
    if only one partner had turned
    and said, 'I'm sorry'?

'I'm sorry.'
Surely it doesn't hurt that much?

Teach me to say, 'sorry', Lord.
To admit when I'm wrong
    and have the courage to admit it,
    even if it does hurt.
To achieve that
    could save a friendship
    a marriage,
    a life.

And, Lord, teach me to forgive,
    to hold no grudges
    even when those concerned
    don't say 'sorry'.

Forgive me, Lord,
    for not saying 'sorry'
    and for not offering forgiveness.
I am sorry.

Amen.

Ha! Ha! Ha!

Intro bit . . .

Where do you start? How can anyone do justifiable praise to this wonderful gift? Where would you begin? An impossible task!

One dream I have quite a lot is that when I get to heaven, Jesus comes up to me with a big smile on his face, hugs me and then asks me to walk with him. We walk and talk for some time, eventually coming to a lake. By the lake is a fire and we sit as he places a few fish on it to cook. He then passes me a bottle of wine, a chunk of bread and smiles. Then, as the glint in his eye shines even brighter, he reminds me of something I did a long time ago and we both start to laugh. And the laughter continues as we eat and drink together by the lake under the setting sun.

Laughing with Jesus? Now *that's* a dream! (Especially if he understands *my* sense of humour!)

Praying bit . . .

> Lord, what's large and white,
>   and if it falls out of a tree
>   can kill you?
>
> A fridge!
>
> Ha! Ha! Ha!
> Yes, Lord, I love laughter.
> It's definitely one of the greatest gifts
>   you've given us.
> There's nothing better
>   than a good rib-tickling,
>   side-aching,
>   eye-crying, laugh!

Laughter can be the best medicine.
You can feel down, upset,
   ill, depressed, alone,
   tired – anything.
But just a small laugh, a quiet giggle,
   and it's all different.
You actually feel better!
Kind of warm inside.

Yep, humour is God-given.
And you, Lord,
I think you've got quite a sense of humour, too.
In fact, I can picture you
   on the shore of Lake Galilee,
   sitting around a small fire,
   cooking fish,
   drinking, and laughing!
Yes, Lord, laughing!

Laughing with Peter, and John,
   laughing with your disciples,
   telling jokes,
   chuckling with each other,
   pulling each other's leg.
Yes, Lord, you laughed!

And you know,
   I can see your sense of humour
   in the world you made.
Take people.
Boy, are there some funny people!
They walk funny, talk funny, dress funny.
Just take a walk down a city street,
   and it's hard not to burst out laughing!

And then there's nature.
Some of your creations
    are truly wonderful and hilarious!
Just watching puppies play,
    lambs running round a field,
    a squirrel eating a hazel nut.
Each one brings a smile.

Yes, Lord, your sense of humour!
What a gift!
Thanks for laughter, Lord,
    it's hilarious!

Amen.

All lies

Intro bit . . .

There can't be anything more damaging than a lie. They niggle at you and eat you away. Your sense of trust diminishes, and you feel empty. Yet, we all lie (and if you say you don't then you just did!) Why? Oh, I guess there are plenty of reasons, from self-preservation to wanting to fit in, but that doesn't make it any better. Jesus calls us to be honest, with him *and* with ourselves. If we can't do either, how can we ever expect to be true to others?

Praying bit . . .

Lord, you there?
Just a word, if you're not busy.
It's just that something's come up.
I didn't expect it.
Not surprising really.

A friend called just now, just to say, 'Hi'.
An innocent face bringing bad news.
Without realising,
    they told me what another 'friend' had done.

I stood there, Lord, kind of stunned.
'My friend lied to me?' I thought.
OK, some people lie without meaning to,
    small, 'unthought-about' lies.
But this, Lord, was carefully thought out,
    planned.

Why not come out with the truth?
Why the need to hide behind a lie?
It hurt, Lord;
 it really hurt.

My friend, Lord,
 whom I remember with affection.
The times we shared, the laughter,
 the happiness, the sadness, the trust.
What now, dear friend?
Why the change of face?
Why turn your back?

Don't you remember me?
Do you really hate me?
Why did you lie?

Lord, you still there?
I suppose, Lord, looking at it,
 the hurt I feel
 is because of all the guilt.
The fact that I've really been the cause of all this.
My fault.

Unwittingly sowing the seeds.
Those few words said in anger.
The talking behind the back.
Yet I knew then, Lord,
 what would happen.
I knew . . .
I saw from the very beginning.

And now, Lord, I come back.
Back to you, my true friend.
The friend who loves
 and forgives me,
 no matter what I do.

Help me to understand
    and forgive my friend, Lord,
    so that I may,
    if only in a small way,
    be like you.

Amen.

Sex!

Intro bit . . .

The church likes bandwagons, and this, I think, is one of them. There are good reasons for this as we all know (see the Ten Commandments!) but sometimes it can turn from loving advice to judgemental condemnation. Jesus calls us to love the Lord our God with all our heart, soul and mind, and to love our neighbours as ourselves. He doesn't expect us to get everything right straight away because he knows us better than we know ourselves. He knows the temptations we face and at the same time forgives. Sex is a beautiful, beautiful gift that should be treated with love, respect and care. Keep it special.

Praying bit . . .

> Lord, can we talk?
> It's about SEX.
> The three-letter word,
>   abused by some,
>   loved by others,
>   the subject of jokes,
>   the cause of giggling
>   in a class of eleven year olds,
>   even the cause of embarrassment.
> All due to one word.
>
> What is it about that small word
>   that scares people?
> It brings them out in a cold sweat!
> They stutter, go red.
> All due to that one word.

To be honest, Lord, so do I.
The trouble is, is that, well, er . . .
    actually, Lord,
    what is the trouble?

Everyone is either male or female,
    their 'sex'.
To produce offspring,
    all species *have* sex.
Couples use sex
    as a way of expressing their love
    for one another.

There!
All wrapped up, neat and tidy!
But it's not that easy, Lord, is it?

Sex is a problem.
First, and most important for me,
    is the 'pre-marital sex' problem.
Lord, I really understand
    why people sleep with each other.
When the lights are low,
    the music soft,
    the two of you are on your own,
    it's hard to say 'no'.

So many people do it.
So many of my friends do it.
It seems to be a part of life,
    completely natural.
But if only they knew.
Lord, sex is a gift from you.
And it's not given
    for the cheap thrill.

Lord, I'd be a liar if I said
   I'd never wanted to sleep with
   someone.
Of course I have!
Everyone has or will do.
We're only human.
The sexual urge is natural, normal.

It's controlling it that's the problem!
If only people were more open,
   more willing to understand.
Many my age think,
   'Well, I've done it now,
   so why stop?'

There's only one reason, Lord:
   I want to save myself
   for that one special person.
I don't want to be there, and say,
   'You're the twentieth person
   I've slept with'.
I want to give that person all of me.

But that's me, Lord.
Where does that leave those
   that have slept around a bit,
   those that feel it's too late?
Have they spoilt something precious,
   and irreplaceable,
   and now can't be forgiven?

Please, Lord, tell them!
Tell them they're not alone,
   that you understand,
   and that they are forgiven.

Help us all, Lord,
    to come to terms
    with sex.
Not to shy away from it,
    not to give in.
But to realise
    how important and beautiful it is,
    to remember how fragile it is,
    and never to forget
    it is your gift to us.

Amen.

Not again!

Intro bit . . .

Exams! Are they horrible, or what? All that revision, all that pressure, all those spare pens, rubbers, rulers and ink cartridges that you won't ever use in a hundred years!

I've had more Grade Es than I'd like to admit. In my family we all take great pride in the fact that four of us (including Dad!) did badly at languages (I got an E for German!) With exams, all you can do is your best, and when the pressure gets too much, when the sun beats down outside making you sweat even more inside, why not have a chat to God about it? After all, he's interested in everything about you!

Praying bit . . .

> Lord, it's happened again!
> Another Grade E
>   and I worked so hard!
> (At least, I think I did).
>
> I did all the research,
>   asked Dad about it,
>   even mentioned it to you,
>   so what went wrong?
> Why an E?
>
> I really thought I'd done well.
> 'I'll show them', I thought.
> But I was wrong,
>   just another bad Grade.

Why is everyone else in the class
    better than me?
Am I thick?
And what's really annoying
    is that they don't even bother about you,
    and yet they still do well!
Why?
It's not fair!

Come on, Lord,
    I know I'm asking for something again,
    but please help me to make
    the next one a bit better.
I want to show them,
    show them that I can do it . . .
    show them that I'm not thick!

And, Lord, if it is another E,
    help me to keep trying,
    and not give up.

(Could I have a D next time, Lord, please . . .)

Amen.

Thanks, Lord

If you get bored one day, get a pen and a pad of paper and start to list all the things you want to say thank you to God for. Don't just stick with the obvious either, like food and sunshine, but go a little bit further. How about saying thank you for the way your biscuits go soggy when you dip them in your tea, or the smell of fresh washing, or posters on your wall . . . you'll probably be there for hours!

Praying bit . . .

> Lord, thank you!
> I just felt I had to say it!
> So many times I've come to you,
>   shouting,
>   screaming,
>   yelling.
> Telling you you're wrong!
> Arguing with you!
> Only bothered about myself,
>   and how I'm feeling.
> Well this time, Lord,
>   I just want to say, 'thanks'.
> Thanks for everything!
>
> For my family, Lord;
>   I do love them.
> They've stuck by me,
>   brought me up.
> I love them, Lord, thanks!

My friends.
Where would I be without them?
OK, we have our arguments,
 but they keep me going,
 talk to me, laugh with me,
 (and at me!)
They make me happy.
Thanks for them, Lord.

Oh, and thanks for music.
I'd go mad without it!
From the hard loud, rock,
 to the soft and thoughtful classical,
 each expressing a different mood,
 be it the desire to jump and dance,
 or the wanting to sit and cry.
Music helps me get through each day,
 express feelings that otherwise
 remain silent.
Music! I love it!

Thanks also, Lord, for the countryside,
 and its beauty.
From the valley to the field,
 the river to the stream,
 the awesome mountains,
 to the soft rolling hills.
Thanks for the wildlife
 that makes it come alive;
 the foxes, rabbits,
 birds, insects.
All of it, Lord,
 pointing to your creative genius.
Such fantastic artwork!
Thanks, Lord!

And thanks also for people.
So much potential,
    in that which is small and vulnerable!
We have the ability to think and learn,
    to create,
    (and sadly, to destroy),
    to love, laugh,
    cry, hear, see.
Lord, I feel I could go on forever,
    the list seems endless!

So much to say thank you for:
    family,
    friends,
    music,
    life,
    countryside,
    love,
    home,
    church,
    wildlife,
    food,
    happiness,
    adventure,
    excitement,
    sport,
    clothes . . .
Lord, I could just keep on going!
But there is just one more thing to add.
Thank you, Lord, for loving me!

Amen.

Love

Intro bit . . .

I decided to do something really grown up the other day. I even got really close to actually doing it, but instead decided it would be much more fun to go and buy a couple of Gerbils! They're great! They live in this massive aquarium in my front room, run around a lot, eat, make tunnels and . . . *cuddle*! It's amazing! These two tiny creatures, these two little balls of fur, spend a little bit of time nearly every minute touching or hugging or preening each other. They even have a greeting that looks like they're kissing!

God's love is everywhere (even in Gerbils!) and if you don't believe me, have a look!

Praying bit . . .

> Lord, it's about 'love'.
> That word,
>   that wonderful four letter word.
> Did you ever realise
>   that it would hold so much power?
> Have so many meanings?
> Can we just think about it
>   for a moment, Lord?
> Because I have to admit
>   that I find it all rather confusing.
>
> LOVE . . .
> What is it, Lord?
> What does it mean?
> For it's used in so many different ways,
>   each one almost contradicting
>   the others.

How many people say 'I love'
   without realising
   the full potential of that word?
For example, Lord,
   I love chocolate,
   and I also love music,
   and going to the theatre.
Yet at the same time
   I also love my family,
   I love my friends,
   I love you!

You see?
I use the same word
   but to mean something different
   each time!
I can hardly compare my love of chocolate
   with the love I have for my family!

And then also, Lord,
   I can think of other situations:
   when, 'I love you' is whispered
   into a loved one's ear,
   or you 'make love' with your partner.

Now there's an interesting thought, Lord!
How do you 'make' love?
Are there special ingredients?
'Leave for 1-2 hours in the oven,
   until brown on top'!

Quite humorous don't you think, Lord?
But maybe not so far from the truth.
You know, Lord,
   I think there are special ingredients
   that make for real love.

Remember that passage
   from the Bible, Lord?

Love is very patient and kind,
   never jealous or envious,
   never boastful or proud,
   never haughty or selfish or rude.
Love does not demand its own way.
It is not irritable or touchy.
It does not hold grudges,
   and will hardly even notice
   when others do it wrong.
It is never glad about injustice,
   but rejoices whenever truth wins out.
If you love someone
   you will be loyal to them
   no matter what the cost.
You will always believe in them,
   always expect the best of them.
And always stand your ground
   in defending them.

(1 Corinthians 13:4-7)

The ingredients of love.
A long recipe for such a small word!

But just as a final request, Lord,
   teach me to love.
To love the way you love
   each and every one of us,
   no matter what we do.
And above all, Lord,
   help me to love you.

Amen.

Friendship

Intro bit . . .

I have some great friends and I do my best to thank God for them every day. We've had some tough times, but we've also had some totally hilarious times! I remember once, when myself and a couple of mates shared a house, Trev (who looks a little like John Travolta!) had gone to bed really early because he had teaching practice in the morning. Well, both me and Marti didn't so we'd been out all night and had rolled in at about one in the morning. A little later, when we were feeling tired, we thought it would be really funny to put Trev's school bag on the small table in the centre of the room and hide it under some stuff. So, that's exactly what we did.

The next morning, Trev was greeted with a mountain of drums, cymbals, furniture, paper, plates and anything else we had managed to get our hands on! He didn't laugh then, but we have done ever since!

Friendship is one of the greatest gifts you will ever have, and one of the greatest gifts you can ever give. Thank God for it now and again, it's worth it.

Praying bit . . .

> Lord, you there?
> I just want to have a chat for a minute.
> It's not really a 'thank you' prayer
>   or a 'questioning' prayer,
>   not even an 'angry'
>   or 'confused' prayer.
> Just a chat.

It's about friendship.
A single word that means so much.
First, Lord, I guess I should say thanks.
You've made my life so full
    of friends and friendship.
Some I've lost contact with,
    some I've drifted away from.
Others I've lost through argument,
    and some were nothing
    but candles in the wind.
But without each of them,
    my life would have been poorer.
Together they've given the happiness,
    guidance, and love that I've needed.
And for that I thank you
    and remember each one before you,
    by each individual name.

Yep, friends are pretty great!

But, Lord, we both know the problems,
    don't we?
How some imagine that friendship
    is easy:
    no problems,
    easy come, easy go.

Not so, Lord!
I've learnt from experience,
    how hard and demanding
    friendships can be.
For each of us is different.
It's not that I'm complaining,
    just recognising that those differences
    often become barriers.
Everyone is going to come across people
    they don't get on with.

The dreaded 'personality clash'!
Believe me, Lord,
   I've met a few that I just can't stand!
Their habits irritate,
   their talk jars (and never stops!)
They get on my nerves,
   discredit what I say,
   and laugh at what I believe.
Lord, there are some people
   I just don't like!

Mind you, I guess I'm as much
   to blame.
I'm stubborn, big-headed,
   loud-mouthed, short-tempered,
   always think I'm right
   and have the answer.
I'm surprised anyone gets on
   at all with me!

But then there are others,
   those I can and do get on with.
They have the same sense of humour,
   similar interests,
   and ideas and beliefs.
I enjoy their company,
   and we become friends.
I guess I have many friends like that,
   'buddies', 'mates',
   call them what you want.
The ones you see at school,
   meet at the youth club.
Friendships you enjoy,
   but that you sadly drift in and
   out of for no other reason
   than you're growing up.

But as you do,
    so the friendship of one or two
    becomes more important.
You talk more,
    learn more about each other,
    and discover the meaning of trust.
And if the friendship
    becomes really special,
    so you come to love each other.
Friends like this, I really thank you for.
Without them, their care and support,
    I'd be lost.

You can have arguments, and fall out,
    but for what has been gained and shared,
    I thank you, Lord.
For each one has taught me just a little
    more about life,
    about people,
    the world,
    and you.
For you are my greatest friend.

Lord, I thank you for friendship,
    and I pray that you will help me,
    not only to appreciate my friends,
    but to be a friend.

Amen.

Boredom

Intro bit . . .

There really is no excuse for this, is there? It's not as if 'finding something to do' is difficult (even if it is the washing up!) There's a great verse in the Bible that goes like this: 'I have come that you may have life, and have it to the full' (John 10:10, NIV). Now is that something, or what? Jesus came so that we could have a really great time! So that we could go crazy about life, live it to the full, party our socks off and not waste a single second of any minute of any hour of any day, ever! So, next time you're bored, don't just sit around and get even more bored. Get off your backside and do something! That's what life is for, so live it!

Praying bit . . .

> Lord,
>   I'm bored!
> Dead bored!
> Totally bored!
> Completely and utterly bored!
>
> B - O - R - E - D!
>
> Bored.
> Nothing to do.
> No one to talk to.
> Nowhere to go.
> Totally bored.
> So I thought we might have a chat.
> I hope you don't mind.

Do you get bored, Lord?
Have times when you've nothing to do?
Just sitting around, kicking your heels,
    doodling on a heavenly bit of paper?

What is boredom, Lord?
Does it really exist?
And if so, why?
There's no reason for it, it's just there.
Just look at this world.

So much to see, so much to do.
When I think about it there's no reason
    to be bored.
In fact I don't think boredom exists!
But *laziness* does!

Laziness, the 'can't be bothered' attitude.
Not bored, just lazy.
Why are we lazy?
Again I can't see any reason for it,
    none at all.
There's so much to do,
    so much needing to be done.
So why is it we can't be bothered?

Lord, save me from my laziness.
Help me not to become bored,
    and forgive me for the excuses I make
    for my laziness, and my boredom.
Show me that there is so much
    to see and do,
    and so little time to achieve any of it.

Lord, stop me from being bored.
It's so boring!

Amen.

Exams

Intro bit . . .

Another prayer on this? Well, why not, it features fairly big in most of our lives and God is interested, even though we may not believe it.

Let me admit something; I'm not an academic type person. I hate sitting and writing essays on questions I'm really not interested in. I hate trying to learn information that my brain refuses to take in. I'd much rather have been climbing or writing a novel or cleaning the toilet than doing exams! But I had to do them, so I did. It'd be nice to be able to offer you some advice, to help you with your revision but I'm sure my way of revising will go with me to the grave and leave the world much better off! All I'll say is that if I can survive, then so can you, so don't give in . . . ever!

Praying bit . . .

> AAAARRRRGGGGHHHH!
> Lord!
> I HATE EXAMS!
> GCSE! A Levels!
> Exams!
> No matter how small or large,
>   important or insignificant,
>   I hate them all!
>
> Revision.
> The dreaded, chilling word
>   that haunts school life!
> 'Revise section one for a test
>   on Monday.'

That feared warning that dispels all
   hopes of a weekend's freedom
   and pleasure!

Lord, did you ever have to do an exam?
Did you ever have to revise?
Did you ever sweat over a pile of books,
   counting the days and hours
   to your appointment with the examiner?

Would you be able to cover everything,
   and know all the answers?
Would you pass?

And what if you didn't?
What then, where could you go?
What could you do?

Lord, the questions run round my brain,
   futile and unnecessary,
   as I try to concentrate.
Wondering all the time if I can pass,
   if I have the slightest chance of success.
Will the examiner be kind?
Will they be able to read my writing?
And worst of all, Lord,
   how much time is there left?
The sacrifices have been made,
   free moments become rare pleasures.
Four hours every night,
   shut away with books,
   writing notes,
   and trying to remember
   without cracking under the strain.
With the thought that the future might
   rest on every moment spent revising,

and wondering why everyone else
seems to achieve more than me.

Is life a big exam, Lord?
Is each day in itself another test?
With the results written in a large
    record book?
The final mark being read out
    as you approach the Pearly Gates.
And what if you fail?

Am I failing, Lord?
I often wonder.
If it is anything like the rest of my exams
    then I don't stand much chance.

Help me, Lord, to be able
    to pass the test,
    to run life's race,
    and never give up.
To do my best – for you.
And, when swamped by a pile of books,
    and confused by countless questions,
    then help me to pause
    and to give thanks
    that in all the stress,
    the work and the pain,
    I have, at least, the opportunity
    to try to do well.
Thank you, Lord, for that.

Amen.

Money and poverty

Intro bit . . .

We all dream of having a bit of money, don't we? Especially when
we see others who are so much richer than us. But if you look at
it, what does it matter? Isn't a £50,000 sports car just a car that
gets to sixty miles per hour three seconds faster than average?
Money is necessary, but it isn't worth what people sometimes do
to get it. You can't take it to heaven, and when you do die, you're
not exactly going to sit around reminiscing about that great stereo
you had once upon a time! More likely you'll remember friends,
family, happy times and the life you've lived, the experiences
you've created. Now they are priceless!

Praying bit . . .

> Lord, I've just been watching TV.
> A millionaire's mansion flashed
>   up on the screen,
>   complete with private swimming pool,
>   tennis courts,
>   limousines,
>   and security guards.
> All that money.
> Is it morally right, Lord?
> For one person to have so much
>   while others have so little?
>
> Believe me, Lord, if I'd worked hard,
>   and made myself a million,
>   I'd want to keep what I'd earned!
> But is that wrong?

Then, Lord, I see other pictures.
I see homeless people on the streets.
I see the tired faces of children
    living in run-down, high-rise flats.
I see the queue of people outside
    the job centre.

The picture changes again,
    as I see another queue,
    only now they stand in line
    waiting for food.

Queueing in hope
    outside an empty shop – the harvest
    has failed for yet another year.

And as their faces fade from view,
    so others come into focus.
I see a desert,
    some threadbare tents,
    and the occupants dying like flies,
    adult and child alike.
Malnutrition, disease, neglect.

The pictures fade,
    and the last thing I see is a child
    with its tiny hand stretched out
    towards me.
Its eyes are covered with flies,
    its impoverished naked body,
    thin and sickly.
In its eyes I see the hurt
    of all who suffer.
'Why?' it whispers, as the picture dims,
    'Why me?'

So I'm brought back
    to my own selfishness,
    my own thoughtless greed.
I realise how lucky I am
    to be where I am.
To have money,
    to have food and clothing,
    to have the opportunity to
    enjoy my future,
    (to even have a future!)
To have the chance to work, and to live.

Lord, please help me.
Help me to realise how fortunate
    I really am.
Help me to make the most
    of my opportunities
    and to stop being ungrateful.
And at the same time
    never let me forget those
    who have so little;
    the poor and the hungry,
    the homeless and unemployed.
And though I may not be able to
    do much to help them, Lord,
    may I do what I can,
    and always remember them in prayer,
    so that they will know that we both care!

Amen.

Music

I profess to be a drummer. I can also hit the keys on a piano in roughly the right order, strum three chords on a guitar and tap away on the bodran (an Irish drum). I'm not very good at any of them, but I do love it! Music is one of the most amazing things ever. Where do all those tunes keep coming from? And all those sounds? Fantastic! I wonder what instrument God plays?

Praying bit . . .

Lord! Hi!
I was just wondering . . .
What's your favourite music?
You see, it just hit me today,
    what a world it'd be without music.
(Where would teenagers be then??!!)
There's so many types,
    so many sounds.
But it's not just sound,
    it's mood,
    thought,
    feeling . . .
An expression of everything,
    condensed into the glory of melody.

Sometimes it makes me want to dance
    (although I'm not much good at it, Lord!)
Other times it fills me with happiness,
    and then in a different mood
    it makes me feel sad.

It can pick me up when I'm down,
    or make me stop and think.

But there's other music too, Lord;
    the music around us –
    the sounds of the earth.
It's as if the world is one large
    concert hall!

The beautiful song of the bird call,
    the *a cappella* of the Morning Chorus,
    the deep bass of the frog's throaty song,
    the unending laughter
    of the bubbling beck,
    the steady beat of the rain,
    the soft rustle of the trees . . .

Lord, there's so much music!
So many sounds and so many players,
    be it bird or hand,
    record deck or river.
I thank you for them all.
And, Lord, thanks for letting me
    be one of the musicians!

Amen.

Me

Intro bit . . .

It can be difficult to like ourselves sometimes, can't it? Especially if we're honest and take a good look at all our bad points. The trouble with this is that we can get wrapped up in not liking who we are, rather than holding Jesus' hand and changing, always reminding ourselves that we are totally and utterly loved by God!

Jesus said, 'Love your neighbour as yourself.' Now, if we don't think much of who we are, then what can we ever offer someone else? If you don't like yourself then you're going to find it fairly hard to like a stranger or even a friend. So next time you look in the mirror, pull a funny face, make yourself laugh and then give yourself a big hug! Learn to love who you are a little more because Jesus said so and loves you too!

Praying bit . . .

> Hi, Lord! It's ME!
> Yes, little old me!
> You know,
> > I've never really thought about it before,
> > but I'd like to say thank you,
> > for ME!
>
> I guess I'm usually so lost
> > in my own self-pity that I forget.
> I forget to look at myself,
> > and stop moaning.
> If I'd only realise what I've got.
> What I am.

So, I'd like to thank you, Lord, for ME!
I know I'm far from perfect,
    but I've still got so much
    to thank you for.
From my little toe on my left foot,
    to my belly-button!
From my sense of humour
    to my smile!
All of it is me,
    your creation, a 'one-off',
    a 'never to be repeated' design,
    a secret mix of ingredients
    to make a totally unique individual.

And that makes me pretty special!
Well, it must, mustn't it?
You see, what I'm trying to say
    is that every part of me,
    biological and psychological,
    is from you.
Your gift to me!
Be it my right arm,
    or my sense of smell
It all adds up to ME!
And being that special, makes me
    feel kind of SPECIAL!!
No one else like me;
    unique
    little old me,
    a one off, by God!
What a thought!

So, Lord, again, all I want to say
    is thank you.
Thank you for ME!

Amen.

Drugs

Intro bit . . .

Everyone knows someone, or of someone, who's either experimented with, or taken, drugs. The whole drugs issue seems to get more and more fuzzy as people argue for the legalisation of Cannabis and so on. All I know is what I've heard from friends and what I've seen with my own eyes; it isn't worth it. God's given us a life to live, not to waste away. It's a gift of immeasurable pricelessness and we should treat it that way, with the respect it demands. Yes there are temptations and many of us will bow to them time and again, but God still loves us, and we should hold onto that, no matter what. And, if in doubt, pray about it!

Praying bit . . .

> Drugs! Why?
> Why do people take them?
> (Can we talk about it, Lord?)
> I just can't understand it.
> Why do they do it?
> They know it destroys them,
>   yet still they crave that 'high'.
> So many lives wasted,
>   thrown away,
>   all because of an exciting kick
>   that became an agonising addiction,
>   a life of imprisonment.
> A sentence of death.
>
> Why, Lord?
> Why do you allow it?

Can't you stop it?
Is it out of your control?
Is there no cure?

But it's not the drug
    that's the real problem, is it, Lord?
There's more to it than that,
    more than can be seen on the surface.
For there's another problem,
    one that's harder to find,
    harder to come to terms with.
The problem is 'us', Lord.

Humanity in all its greatness,
    its striving for power,
    for a better life,
    a more advanced technology,
    has forgotten the little people.
The people who couldn't keep up,
    couldn't run the race,
    and got left behind.
And instead of waiting, Lord,
    humanity just kept on going,
    leaving them in its wake;
    the unwanted,
    the poor,
    the homeless,
    the hungry . . .
    the drug addict.

For them this was a final grasp
    at happiness;
    drugs became 'the friend',
    always there,
    easy to reach,
    easy to enjoy.

At last – happiness in a needle.

And they forgot about the pain,
    the addiction,
    the disease,
    DEATH!

Lord, help me,
    for confronted
    with such a problem,
    I feel lost and inadequate.
I don't even know how to pray about it.
For what is the solution?
Is there a cure?
I want to see the problem solved.
I want to find an answer,
    but I don't even know what to ask for.
How can I fight the war on drugs?

Let's be honest, Lord, I can't.
But in all my helplessness,
    I can still pray,
    and feel the need to pray,
    in the hope that, though small,
    it may help.
Lord, please, hear this, my prayer.

Amen.

Hurting inside

Intro bit . . .

How many times have you had to fake the way you feel to others? You know, smile at them and laugh and join in, even though inside you're breaking up?

There's one person you'll never be able to do that to because all he sees is the real you. He even feels your pain. So often we pray for help, pray for forgiveness but continue to feel no different. We wallow in our guilt, almost happy to stay unhappy. We forget that once we have asked for forgiveness then we are forgiven! That's it! The slate is clean! Yes, there are consequences if we sin or do wrong, but to be able to say 'I'm forgiven!' How wonderful and freeing is that?

Guilt often stays because we refuse or maybe feel unable to let it go. The only way round this is to keep going, to hold on and eventually the hurting on the inside will heal.

Praying bit . . .

Lord, are you there?
I feel like I'm dying inside.
On the outside I'm fine,
    everything's cheery,
    not a care in the world.
But inside, Lord, oh, that's different.
A lot different!
Where has all the laughter gone?
The joy,
    the happiness of the life
    I used to know?
Has it completely gone, Lord,
    out of reach?

For I need it, Lord,
    that fire which burned so strong,
    that now only smoulders,
    burning embers of a distant memory,
    disappearing on the lonely wisp
    of dusty smoke.

Lord, are you listening?
I'm really beginning to wonder.
What is it all about?

I've changed so much, Lord.
But I'm hurting.
My heart is beginning to feel the strain.

Are you wanting this to happen, Lord?
Is it part of your 'Great Plan'?
My faith used to be so strong.
I lived for you,
    loved you.
Yet now . . .?

Now I'm drifting.
I'm confused, unstable,
    with nothing to hold on to.
I have a friend, Lord.
The greatest gift you ever gave.
Someone I trust, and care for
    like no other.
But am I loosing him too?
I'm not angry, Lord,
    he needed what has been given.
But I'm jealous.
Not of him, Lord,
    not of you.
Just jealous.

He is so happy,
    yet the happiness he has
    is still out of my reach.

So again I'm feeling alone.
It's so easy to say,
    'With you I'll never be alone'.
But I'm only human.
How much am I meant to take
    before breaking?
I'm fighting, Lord, but I can't win.
Much more, and I don't think
    I'll get up again.
Can't you see that, Lord?
Hasn't there been enough heartbreak?
Isn't it about time you picked me up,
    out of this choking dust?

Please?

Amen.

Life

Intro bit . . .

Life is fantastic! It's amazing! It's totally and utterly the best thing ever! I am lost for words, unable to describe how completely in love I am with the whole idea of life and being alive! I love it, I live it and I thank God for it! Perhaps some of us should get together sometime and just have a huge worldwide party to celebrate 'life'!

Praying bit . . .

>Hi, Lord, can we talk?
>Just a little 'thank you'.
>My life, I'm loving it.
>(Well, at the moment anyway!) It's great.
>There's so much to do,
>   so many things to see.
>It's so exciting.
>
>I know there are hard times.
>Times I feel like giving up,
>   jacking it all in.
>Times when it seems
>   the world's against me,
>   and everything's going wrong.
>But if I just sit back,
>   then I see that things aren't so bad after all.
>It's all had a purpose,
>   helped me to grow up in some small way.
>And it even seems
>   that there's a direction to it all.
>
>Are you guiding me, Lord?
>Only it doesn't seem very obvious.

Is there a path you want me to follow?
Is there a way I should take?
(Could I have a map, Lord?)

It's like being on a big expedition,
    the greatest adventure ever.
Round every corner there are
    new things to discover, new places to see,
    new people to meet, new things to do.
And like every expedition,
    you need to be prepared,
    have the right equipment to survive.
And you've even thought that through, Lord.

The most obvious need is a map,
    or a guidebook,
    and what more could we ask for – the Bible,
    THE Guide Book!
Every page answers questions,
    poses problems,
    makes me think,
    shows me the Way.

And for any expedition,
    you also need a Guide,
    someone to interpret,
    to help you understand the Map,
    someone who knows the Way,
    a person who's been there – you, Lord,
    the best guide in the world!

And that's it.
What an adventure!
You and the Guide Book to show us the Way!

LET'S GO!

Amen.

Am I a Christian?

Intro bit . . .

That's a good question, isn't it? I ask myself that every day and the answer, I often find, is only vaguely 'yes'. I don't feel worthy to wear that name. I don't see how it is possible that I ever could; it seems so far beyond my reach. Yet Jesus said that if we accept him as our Lord and Saviour then we are saved, and I for one am going to listen to him. No matter what happens or however bad things get, I'm not going to give in. Ever. Jesus loves me and I am saved! End of story!

Praying bit . . .

> Lord, can we talk?
> It's about my faith,
>   my belief.
> You see, as a Christian
>   I'm supposed to 'spread the Word',
>   'tell the Good News',
>   'bring people to Christ'.
>
> To be honest, Lord, I don't,
>   (well at least, not very well).
> I'm nervous, scared, embarrassed.
> 'What will people think?'
> 'I can't tell them, they'll laugh at me.'
>
> It's quite a problem
>   because for some reason
>   people ask, 'Are you a Christian?'

'YES!' I proclaim out loud!
But then they ask, 'Why?'
And that finishes me,
    I'm done for,
    trapped,
    a stuttering mass of confusion,
    lost for words,
    and unable to answer.
Huh! Some Christian!

I do know why I believe.
(Honest!)
It's just explaining it that's the problem.
Can you give me some help, Lord?
How about a job description,
    guidelines for nervous Christians
    things to do,
    and not to do,
    when confronted by that 'why?'

I really wish I could hold my ground,
    answer their every question,
    speak your truth,
    proclaim your Word.
Aren't I good enough?
Am I a bad design?
A faulty product?
What am I doing wrong?

Lord, (are you still there?),
    could you give me a hand, please?
I do find it hard to speak out.
So help me when someone asks,
    'Are you a Christian?'
Because maybe if they're asking,

their reason for doing so
might be me,
my life,
and the way I live it with you.
So who knows, Lord,
maybe I'm getting there after all!

Amen.

Another day over

Intro bit . . .

I love bed! Going to bed, sinking in between those sheets, under
the heavy douvet . . . ahh, it's heaven! Total and utter heaven!
And one of the best things about it? Looking back over the day
and chatting to God about it, sorting out the things that went
wrong, praising him for the things that went right and thanking
him for the things that had every chance of going wrong but didn't!
Oh, and the end of one day means that the next is drawing even
closer! Brilliant!

Praying bit . . .

> Well, Lord, that's another day over.
> Can we talk?
> I've a few things on my mind,
>   a few things I need to say.
>
> First, I'm sorry,
>   for as with every other day,
>   today I've done some things wrong.
> In fact, I've done a lot of things wrong,
>   and sadly,
>   most of the time,
>   I'm not even aware of it.
> Lord, I hope I haven't hurt anyone,
>   or caused too much trouble.
> I guess I'll find out tomorrow.
> Help me to accept criticism,
>   judgement, punishment,
>   and help me to learn from my mistakes.

I'd also like to say 'thanks', Lord.
I've quite enjoyed today.
It's good just to be alive,
    seeing friends,
    being outside,
    laughing;
Thanks, Lord.

And then, can I pray for others too, Lord.
It's just that I saw a few friends today,
    who need help.
Could you give them a hand,
    help them get sorted out
    and make sense of things?

And finally, can you help me
    make tomorrow a bit better than today?
I don't want to keep messing things up.
Could you give me a hand as well, Lord?

Goodnight.

Amen.

Have another

Intro bit . . .

Well, here is a subject I'm an expert on! I can't even begin to imagine how many drinks I've had that have been both stupid *and* enjoyable! But then there's the hangovers, and the jet-propelled vomit, and the headaches, and the not being able to eat anything for days. Yep, I'm an expert all right.

What frightens me though, is how easy it is to become blasé about it. And I don't mind admitting that there have been times when I've been like that.

Alcohol can be amusing and, in the right atmosphere with the right people, it's fine. But it's like anything; enjoy it in moderation rather than excess.

Praying bit . . .

> Lord, can we have a chat?
> It's about alcohol.
> Beer,
>   wine,
>   scotch,
>   gin,
>   and all the rest of it.
> Alcohol.
>
> Why do I drink too much of it?
> Every time, I say to myself,
>   'No more.
> Don't get drunk'.
> But I do.
> My head starts swimming,

I find it hard to stand,
and suddenly everyone else is
laughing at me.

OK, I'll be honest
    it can be fun,
    a good sensation,
    but it's still scary,
    not being in total control.
And then, there's always tomorrow!
The headache,
    the nausea,
    the sickness,
    and the 'wish I was dead' feeling!
And so I say to myself,
    'Never again',
    only to forget it
    the next time round.

Lord, help me to resist,
    to say, 'No',
    to go against the crowd,
    and not just do what they do.

Lord, let my next drink be enjoyable,
    not stupid.

Amen.

Like a thief in the night

Intro bit . . .

God can be scary, can't he? Well, he's God and very powerful so I guess it comes with the territory.

This bit, the Second Coming, has always scared me though because I've always got that niggly feeling that when Jesus does come back he isn't going to take me with him. But at the same time I have to depend on the little faith that I do have. That faith that he does love me and that I am valued and held close and saved. So, when he does come . . .

Praying bit . . .

> Lord, can we talk?
> I'm a bit scared,
>   in fact, I'm very scared.
> It's the 'Second Coming'
>   that's on my mind,
>   your return to earth.
>
> I find it frightening,
>   that you could come at any time,
>   even now while I'm praying.
> 'Like a thief in the night',
>   the Bible says.
> We don't even know when,
>   or where,
>   or how.
>
> How will it happen, Lord?
> The 'thief in the night' thing

gives me the impression it will be
quick and quiet,
and very sudden.

Will you just take Christians?
Will they just disappear?
And what about the rest;
   those you don't take?
Will you give them another chance?
Or is that it?
All over.
The gates of heaven finally locked?

Lord, why can't you just appear?
Now.
Prove you are who you say you are.
Wouldn't it be easier?
You'd have the world at your feet.
But, Lord, who am I to question
   your plans?

Lord, I am frightened.
You see, I don't think I'm good enough
   and I'm afraid you'll leave me behind.
Help me to be ready,
   to be prepared.
Because when you come again
   I don't think I'll have a second chance.

Amen.

Feeling down

Don't you hate it when you wake up and feel really low? There's no reason, you just feel like that. Life suddenly feels like a total drag, a real pain. Nothing you can do can change it, everything is a waste of time, no one cares, what's the point anyway, and to be honest you doubt whether God exists at all.

We all get like this. I know I do. It's not nice but it happens and for any amount of reasons, usually ones you never realised could be the cause. But that's life. Life has ups and it has downs, if it didn't then the highs wouldn't be high!

God gave us freedom but also said he'd walk with us every step of the way, no matter what. And when he seems so far away it's usually because we have made it that way. Yet God is still there, banging on the door we've closed, waiting for us to open it again.

Praying bit . . .

> Lord, I've got to talk.
> You got a minute?
> It's just that I'm feeling down,
>   and I don't know why.
>
> Why am I unhappy?
> I've great friends, parents,
>   music, you, life.
> What could be wrong?
> I don't know, I just feel down.
>
> I'm sick of being taken for granted
>   and ignored.
> 'Oh, Dave doesn't mind.'

'Dave's OK, he'll listen.'
'He's a good laugh, is Dave.'
I'm not OK!

Why don't people realise?
I'm waiting for someone to come along
    and look a little deeper.
To peel away the make-up
    and look at the real me.
I'm lonely, Lord, so lonely.
Yes, I've friends,
    but it's a different kind of loneliness.
The kind that haunts you in a crowd,
    jumps on you
        when you're with a friend.
Stabs you in the back
    when you're by yourself.

So many times I've wanted to scream,
    and reach out for someone.
Someone to hold,
    someone with the loving support
    I need so much.
That tiny bit of affection,
    a genuine love that asks nothing more of me
    than what I have.

Yet, when I reach out
    it's gone.
A shadow in the darkness.

Why is it, Lord?
I'm sorry, but I can't understand.
Why me?
What have I done?
Why can't I show my inner self?
That part of me so few have seen.

The quiet, understanding me,
   the caring, loving me,
   the happy, warm me.
What am I doing wrong?
Does anyone understand?
I'm feeling alone again, Lord.
Left alone in the dark
   as my friends move on.

Why won't they look over their shoulders?
See me kneeling in the dust,
   crying, hurt?
Don't they reallse, Lord?
I want to cry, but I can't.
What do I do?
Shout for them to stop?

Help me, Lord.
I'm so frightened, lost, alone.
Help me, Lord.
I love you,
   but does anyone really love me?

My child,
   don't you remember
   my footsteps in the sand?
When there was only one set
   you asked me why I had left you?
Can't you remember, my child,
   I then carried you!
My love for you is unending,
   so do not worry.
Lean on my love and trust me.
I will carry you
   when you grow weary.

Amen.

Death

I'm not too keen on this, but then I can't think many people are. You don't exactly wake up in the morning and yell, 'Wow! Great! I might die today!'

Death is scary, but it is also something that will happen to us all and Jesus tells us not to be afraid of it. You may have had pets or relatives or even close friends die and that can make it even more real, even more frightening. But if we cling to Jesus and his promise of eternal life, perhaps that fear will slowly but surely diminish.

Praying bit . . .

> Lord, you got a minute?
> It's just that I'm a bit bothered,
>   about death.
> Such a horrible word.
> The dreaded cloaked skeleton,
>   carrying his scythe.
> But why is it such a fearful thing?
> Everyone dies, sooner or later,
>   so what's the problem?
>
>
> Well, with me, Lord,
>   it's because it is certain.
> That for me is frightening.
> No matter what happens
>   one thing's for sure;
>   I will die.

Just the thought
    raises all manner of questions.
How will I die?
Will it be painful?
When will it happen?
What will be the cause?
What happens once I'm dead?

You see, God,
    two lads I've known,
    both my age,
    have died this year.

One killed in a motor bike accident,
    the other died of asthma.
And that really brought it home.
They no longer exist on this earth.
They're gone.
Just memories.
It really made me think.
Are they with you now, Lord?
Do you hold them close?

Lord, this heaven and hell business
    is so hard to understand.
I have so many friends I love
    that I know aren't Christians.
Will you condemn them?
Will you,
    lover of each and everyone of us,
    condemn those who don't believe?
Don't you think that's a bit off?
Evil in fact?
Unjust?
And how, Lord, are you going
    to distinguish me from them?

OK, Lord, I believe in you,
   and I do my best to follow you.
But I can be disgusting,
   a bad example of Christianity.
Doing things that are wrong,
   'sinning without thinking'.

Why do you love me, Lord?
I've sometimes wondered if you do.
Will I die only to be cast into hell?
Does anyone really deserve that?
Do they, Lord?

David, of course I love you,
   I love everyone.
If you only knew how much!
If one is lost, my heart bleeds.
If one is saved, all of heaven rejoices!
Let me worry about everyone else.
I'm just saying to you,
'Follow me'.

Amen.

Discrimination

Intro bit . . .

Everyone experiences discrimination, whether you're old, young, black, white, short, tall, tattooed or not. Discrimination exists and is something we should all fight against. Why?

Simple. Jesus invites *all* to come to him because in him all are made equal. We are all made in the image of God so no matter where we come from, what we believe, what we do or what colour we are, under God we are equal and loved. God loves us all, so why don't we follow his lead?

Praying bit . . .

> Lord, can we talk?
> Something's bothering me.
> It's beginning to make me feel a bit upset.
> What do people think of me, Lord?
> Do they really like me?
> You see I heard something today.
> Something someone had said about me.
> It wasn't really all that nice, Lord.
> It was from a friend.
>
> Why do people do that?
> Why be two-faced?
> Just because I was a bit different.
> Mind you, I guess everyone's guilty.
> Judging only on the little I see.
> If someone is serious,
>   then they are depressing.
> If someone is happy and full of jokes,
>   then they love themselves.

If someone is proud of something
    they've done,
    then they are big-headed.

See what I mean, Lord?
People jump to conclusions.
Just because of the way someone
    is different to you.
Then you don't like them.

It's not just small things either.
Colour,
    race,
    sex,
    belief,
    age.
All make people different.
All cause problems.

I must admit, Lord, that being white
    I don't really know what it's like
    to be on the receiving end of racism.
To be singled out because you're black.
To be hated because of your colour.

So wrong, Lord, so wrong.
So why does it happen?
It's like a disease.
Discrimination.
Labelled because you're different.
No one is left untouched.
It spreads through society.
Every age,
    sex,
    colour,
    race.

Apartheid in South Africa.
Blacks oppressed.
Why?
Because they're black.

Sexism from both sides.
Each thinking they're better than the other.
What happened to Equality?

Anti semitism.
Jews blamed for the downfall of Germany.
A scapegoat.
Genocide.

Ageism.
People aren't employed
    because they're too old.
All youngsters are vandals.

And the list goes on, Lord.
Sad really.
So much hate.
So little reason.

Lord, it's such a huge problem.
I feel out of my depth thinking about it.
Help me not to discriminate.
just because someone is different.
Help me to realise we are all equal.

All human.
All loved.
By you.

Amen.